A DRINKER'S GU[illegible]E TO

CA[illegible]F

.FFEG

A Drinker's Guide to Cardiff
Published by Graffeg © 2014
ISBN 9781909823099

Text © Oliver Hurley
Photographs by Phil Jones

Graffeg Limited,
24 Stradey Park Business
Centre, Mwrwg Road,
Llangennech, Llanelli,
Carmarthenshire SA14 8YP
Wales UK Tel 01554 824000
sales@graffeg.com
www.graffeg.com

Designed and produced by
Graffeg Limited

Distributed by the Welsh Books
Council www.cllc.org.uk
castellbrychan@cllc.org.uk
A CIP Catalogue record for this book is available from the British Library

Thanks to Robbie Bennie,
Jess Hibbert and Kirsty Lyons

CONTENTS

OLIVER HURLEY

Oliver Hurley wrote the words. Contrary, in all likelihood, to the impression given elsewhere in this book, he earns a living through journalism. Despite having contributed to a slew of newspapers, magazines and websites over the years, the only publication that has ever stiffed him is a certain local listings mag, which has owed him £30 since 1998. The proudest moment of his career was when Steve-O ended an interview by asking him, "God, how dumb are you, dude?" He is the author of *Wrestling's 101 Strangest Matches* (Pitch Publishing) and currently works for an interiors magazine, which may explain his fixation with lampshades. He will happily consume any lager that doesn't start with the letter C.

PHIL JONES

Phil Jones took the photos. By day, he works for a dental supplies firm and once provided a performance artist with the surgical equipment necessary to sew his own lips together. By night, he dons a mask and cape while dabbling in freelance photography. He has taken pictures for a variety of magazines, including *The Big Issue*, *Skin Deep*, *Power Slam* and *Loaded* (not those sort of pictures). He can consume up to 12 pints of lager during a single session but has had to give up tea as it gives him heartburn. Go figure.

INTRODUCTION

A Drinker's Guide to Cardiff is based on an idea first explored in a website (pintof45.blogspot.com) that photographer Phil Jones and I launched back in 2008. It was apparent to us that there was a gap for a blog about Cardiff pubs and bars that combined fly-on-the-wall pics with write-ups that were a bit more playful and subjective than the sort of sober (in both senses) approach you find in much pub and beer writing, which can make going out for a drink sound like the most chin-strokingly tedious activity ever conceived.

We weren't particularly interested in what real ales were on tap or whether the food was any good: it was more like an exercise in what would happen if Hunter S. Thompson went on a pub crawl with The Three Stooges. The result was a cavalcade of (sometimes only slightly exaggerated) stories of downing huge amounts of cheap lager – and a lot of hangovers.

This book distils (ahem) a selection of these weird, wonderful and wonky despatches from the frontline into the eminently portable volume you have in your hands now. In most cases we revisited the establishments in question, not only to bring the snapshots and first-hand reports bang up to date – but also because

it was the perfect excuse for a frankly epic bender. Think of this as
part guidebook and part cautionary tale.

This isn't a run-down of Cardiff's 'best' boozers (an impossible notion anyway, given that it depends entirely on what you're looking for) but, instead, is a celebration of the huge variety of hostelries the city has to offer: old-fashioned ale houses, cavernous chain pubs, cheap 'n' cheerful student haunts, glorious beer gardens, idiosyncratic free houses… and whatever the hell The Bunker is.

If our booze-fuelled misadventures have taught us anything, it's that there's something to like about all these places – and that, whether you're after a quick drink after work or a night of rampant hedonism, the Welsh capital doesn't disappoint.

Pint, anyone?

THE ALBANY

105 Donald Street, Roath, Cardiff, CF24 4TL
029 2031 1075 • sabrain.com/albany

That's what a pub should look like, isn't it?

This has everything you want from a bar: a selection of cold lagers, some freshly polished brass (er, that sounds odder than it's meant to), a few bags of peanuts, an emetic line-up of garishly hued concoctions, an extravagantly facial-haired barman doing the hokey-cokey.

The place is decorated in pretty much every shade of brown you'd find in a Pantone colour chart. As, indeed, all traditional boozers should be. And it's got plenty of those little round tables and stools that you only ever see in proper pubs.

Through a corridor to the lounge, where there's some serious telly watching going on. You've rarely seen a group of blokes so rapt in the *EastEnders* omnibus.

Amazingly, The Albany's beer garden does actually constitute being referred to as a garden. You can't beat a nice bit of foliage with your pint.

THE CITY ARMS

10-12 Quay Street,
Cardiff, CF10 1EA
029 2064 1913 •
thecityarmscardiff.com

There's been some sort of public house on this site since the 1850s, when there was an establishment here called The Van of Flesh Tavern. Which is possibly the greatest name for a boozer ever.

It's a bit like a TARDIS in reverse: it's a lot bigger on the outside than it is on the inside. They've managed to cram plenty of grog behind the bar though, including about 293 varieties of cask ale (or thereabouts). If you can't decide what to plump for, you can order a selection of three third-pints of ale – attractively presented on a little plank.

The City Arms is a pub's pub – the acme of alehouses. It's the sort of traditional city centre dram shop that's perfect for a spot of drinking and thinking: you can be pretty sure your pint's not going to be disturbed by screaming brats in three-wheeled buggies or Lady Gaga records played at tinnitus-inducing volume.

Round the corner and you come to this little nook, festooned with yet more beer-related ephemera. The ideal spot to take the weight off your feet while enjoying your booze-plank.

THE FORESTERS

181 Cowbridge Road East, Canton, Cardiff, CF11 9AJ • 029 2025 1801

Before you even make it through the door of The Foresters, you're overwhelmed by a cavalcade of entertainment options. Sky Sport (just the one sport, mind), karaoke, disco, pool, darts… how much fun is it possible to have in a single pub? I'm about to find out.

First things first though: lager. A pleasing golden hue there, reassuring condensation on the glass, slightly foamy head but nothing to be overly concerned about, all speedily delivered. But more importantly – how many sides does this bar have? A lot.

The hostelry has a certain rough charm all of its own. Indeed, the way the words 'Carlsberg Extra' have been proudly daubed on the blackboard above the bar seems to suggest that we're meant to consider such a beverage to be the pinnacle of grog-based exoticism.

One good thing about The Foresters is that they always put health and safety – if not spelling – first.

No sign of the promised disco or karaoke, unfortunately. Although it is only 4.15pm – and even I'm not ready to disco at that time of day.

GOLDEN CROSS

282 Hayes Bridge Road, Cardiff, CF10 1GH
029 2022 5270 •
sabrain.com/golden-cross

The Golden Cross – a proper bit of old Cardiff and one of the region's most popular gay pubs – is just round the corner from the swish cathedral of consumerism that is the new bit of St David's shopping centre. But it might as well be in another world. For starters, where did you last see net curtains like that? Not in the John Lewis home furnishings department, that's for sure.

There's an impressive selection – some would say an overload – of lagers, including Peroni, full-strength Stella and, hilariously, both Foster's and Carling. As if anyone can actually tell the difference between the two.

The intricately detailed ceramic bar dates from the 19th century. I'm more interested in the expansive stash of booze behind it though, which appears to include 75 per cent of south Wales' entire stock of Jägermeister.

The children's menu on the wall features a truly chilling rendition of a clown's head – it's like something out of a Stephen King novel. The bloke in the red T-shirt can't even bring himself to look at it.

The place hosts regular karaoke and cabaret nights. Although, to be honest, that's less of a stage, more of a large upturned box.

THE ANDREW BUCHAN

29 Albany Road, Roath, Cardiff, CF24 3LH
theandrewbuchan.com

I know what you're thinking. "That is one weird pub. It almost looks as if it used to be a video rental store or something." And you'd be right. It is a weird pub and it used to be a video rental store (Choices, to be precise).

➡ It's operated by Rhymney Brewery – so, in addition to your Strongbows and Carlsbergs, you've got the well-priced delights of the baldly-named Rhymney Bitter, Rhymney Dark, Rhymney Export et al. Although whether transporting something from Blaenavon to Roath really constitutes 'export' remains to be seen.

There's something about the place that makes it feel like a set, as if the walls might start wobbling at any moment.

Wouldn't it be great if they fed the chimney from that wood-burner into the back of this fella's head in order to pump smoke out its mouth? Now that would draw the punters in, surely: "Come and enjoy a pint while marvelling at Albany Road's famous smoke-belching moose!"

Talking of smoke belching, the smoking area is so bizarre that Louis Theroux is currently making a documentary about it.

BUNK HOUSE

93-94 St Mary Street,
Cardiff, CF10 1DX
029 2022 8587 •
bunkhousecardiff.co.uk

There's plenty going on at this hostel-cum-drinkery, as the signage confirms. Although surely the correct order of events should be: 'Bar. Boogie. Beds.' Doing the 'beds' bit first makes no sense at all.

◀ Step inside and it's a carnival of bunting, fairy lights and picnic tables adorned with tasseled, sunflower-yellow parasols. Wetherspoon it ain't.

➡ You can't help but be impressed by the fact that the bloke in the kilt remains resolutely unperturbed by the luridly coloured, miniature seating arrangement to his right.

⬅ If heading to the dorms upstairs seems like too much of an effort at the end of a grievous night on the tiles, there's a handy arrangement of beds and chaises longues directly opposite the bar, replete with chintzy quilts and cushions covered in vintage fabrics. Although the chances are you'll wake up in the morning and wonder what the hell you're doing in your nan's front room.

⬇ The cause of – and solution to – all life's ills. (Well, most of them.)

GWDIHŴ

6 Guildford Crescent, Cardiff, CF10 2HJ
029 2039 7933 •
gwdihw.co.uk

Unless you're staying at the Ibis hotel over the road, Gwdihŵ isn't a place you're likely to stumble across. Which is a shame. After all, where else in the 'Diff will you find a bright orange cantina with an owl motif perched above the door?

When the place first opened, there was as much of an emphasis on serving sandwiches as there was on dispensing hooch. Fortunately, they've since righted that wrong – eating is cheating, after all – and you can get the party started with everything from Czech lager Kozel to craft beers by local brewery Pipes, via an arsenal of spirits and cocktails.

Nothing will quite prepare you for the, shall we say, hectic design aesthetic that assaults you when you step inside. It's reminiscent of a particularly experimental episode of *Changing Rooms* – you know, where the people whose house it is burst into tears when they see what Laurence Llewelyn-Bowen has done to their front room.

Sort of like the *Mona Lisa*, this. Wherever you stand, it's always looking at you.

PORTER'S

Harlech Court, Bute Terrace, Cardiff, CF10 2FE
029 2125 0666 • porterscardiff.com

From the outside, Porter's may well be a nondescript-looking establishment in an unlikely location (it's tucked away on Bute Terrace between The Big Sleep hotel and an immense block of flats). But its delights are many and varied.

➧ For one, it's home to Cardiff's smiliest bar person.

The well-curated array of beers includes Blue Moon, Brooklyn Lager, Modelo, Anchor Steam Beer and this 8.4% Belgian concoction, Pauwel Kwak. So that patrons aren't tempted to nick the shapely receptacle, you're asked to leave a shoe behind the bar as security. The photographer, haggler extraordinaire that he is, manages to reduce the deposit down to a hat. One (presumably hatless) woman was once so reluctant to remove a shoe that she instead left her wedding ring behind the bar. Which perhaps doesn't bode particularly well for her marriage.

A side room houses this bijou cinema – themed screenings of a trio of films take place every Sunday. Although due to some sort of licensing quirk, the bar isn't allowed to advertise which films it's showing outside the premises.

Keep going through the cinema and you arrive at this mini golf course. Which if it wasn't for the photographic evidence to the contrary, I'd be convinced I had imagined after one Kwak too many.

THE BUNKER

60-61 St Mary Street,
Cardiff, CF10 1FE
029 2022 6802 •
thebunkercardiff.co.uk

The Bunker is, ostensibly, a sports bar. But in both name and presentation it's more like a fortified compound in which to take shelter from the impending apocalash. (Otherwise known as a Saturday night on St Mary Street.)

◀ It does a fine line in beverages that no one has ever heard of. Indeed, Backyard Retro sounds more like some sort of seizure-inducing moonshine than it does a legitimate lager-based product.

➧ The 'sports' aspect of proceedings comprises some darts on the telly (which, let's be honest, is a game not a sport) and the fact that there is enough open space to accommodate gymnastic floor routines. Which is, it transpires, what those three blokes on the left are limbering up for.

➧ The gymnastics judges go on to have a rather heated discussion about scores at the bar. It's a close call but, in the end, Jester-Hatted Bloke gets the nod and is through to next week's live final.

➧ This is The Blue Room. What happens in The Blue Room stays in The Blue Room.

DEMPSEYS

15 Castle Street,
Cardiff, CF10 1BS
029 2023 9253 •
sabrain.com/dempseys

Now this is a pub. It's painted an indistinguishable hue best described as 'murky', it sells decent beer, it has an unappealing outside area that basically involves sitting on the street, it plays great music and, erm, it smells a bit funny. What's not to love?

All the usual Brains suspects are on offer, although it's Brains Smooth that takes pride of place. That's not so much a beer tap as a fluorescent totem pole that's been hardwired into the national grid.

➧ For some reason, going to Dempseys during the day just feels wrong, wrong, wrong – as if it's only really appropriate to be here if you're actively engaged in night-time carousing.

➧ Speaking of which. Indeed, given that it's open till 3am on Fridays and Saturdays, it's the ideal spot for bringing a serious session to a close. They don't seem to mind too much if you're visibly inebriated and the music – which is heavy on the indie-disco classics – will sort you right out even if you're starting to flag.

➧ There is this alarming corridor, though, which promises a 'bathroom and toilet'. Suffice to say that, whatever the sign says, anyone coming to a Cardiff city centre, Irish-themed alehouse looking for a bathroom is going to leave sorely disappointed.

THE LIVE LOUNGE

9 The Friary, Cardiff, CF10 3FA
029 2132 8159 • thelivelounge.com

If you've ever been accosted in Cardiff by a trilby-adorned unicyclist dishing out flyers, this is the watering hole he's promoting. According to the signage, it's a 'bar, restaurant and coffee shop'. Which, admittedly, does sound better than 'cut-price booze warehouse'.

➧ Friday night crowd. Note shaven-headed chap in foreground sporting the rather avant-garde prop of a pair of upside-down sunglasses perched at the back of his head. It's what the Invisible Man looks like when he gets dressed in a hurry.

The Live Lounge's USP is the identity parade of covers bands that perform here. Covers bands, that is, with names such as Right Said Fred West, 4Play, The Groovinators and Minnie's Chuff. Imagine phoning up the venue to arrange a gig. "And what's your band called, mate?" "Minnie's Chuff." "Ha ha, brilliant. You're booked."

The walls are strewn with portraits of the likes of Kings of Leon, The Cure, Manic Street Preachers, Slash and Michael Jackson. Almost as a constant visual reminder that none of these performers will ever play here. Especially Michael Jackson. Obviously.

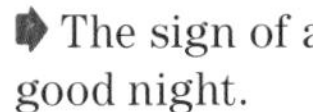

The sign of a good night.

REVOLUCIÓN DE CUBA

The Friary, Cardiff, CF10 3FA
029 2000 8444 • revoluciondecuba.com/bar/cardiff

What better way to commemorate an armed revolt that took place on a Caribbean island in the 1950s than via the medium of a themed drinks emporium in the centre of the Welsh capital?

➧ It's billed as a 'rum bar'. Or, as we used to call them back in the day, a 'rough pub'. Ahem. Good place for a mojito, though.

The thoughtful layout incorporates two large bars at opposite ends of the room and there's plenty of space in between for both drinkers (this is a good destination if you're in a large group) and diners.

Friday night revellers Havana laugh.

Ironically, given the size of the room, the live music doubles as an exercise in finding out how many band members you can squeeze into as small a space as possible. Quick, someone get Norris McWhirter on the phone. (Apologies to anyone not familiar with 1980s children's telly, for whom that reference will be completely baffling.)

MILGI

213 City Road, Roath, Cardiff, CF24 3JD
029 2047 3150 • milgilounge.com

Being wedged between a Conservative club (surely the worst of all the clubs) and an outlet for discount printer cartridges isn't an obvious location for a hipstery, vegetarian cafe-bar.

➧ The mismatched furniture, colourful tablecloths and assorted knick-knacks give the interior something of a retro tea room aesthetic. With, er, added plywood moose head. It's perhaps the most unlikely location in Cardiff in which you can order cans of Red Stripe.

Out the back is where the real action is, though. You know your merrymaking has taken a turn for the surreal when the scenery includes a decommissioned dodgem as flower bed.

Psychedelic Triceratops mural. Standard.

Nice pineapples.

And then obviously there's this enormous, disco ball-equipped yurt – quite possibly the only one on City Road. To be honest, it's a lot to cope with after you've been at the Red Stripe all afternoon.

THE PEN & WIG

1 Park Grove, Cathays, Cardiff, CF10 3BJ
029 2037 1217 • penandwigcardiff.co.uk

I've always liked The Pen & Wig. I once bumped into the manager on the beach in Minehead at about five in the morning (it's a long story), which only served to endear the place to me further.

➧ It's tucked away just off St Andrew's Place and is a favourite with students and the slew of legal professionals who work nearby. You would hope they don't get too carried away with that 7.3% Old Rosie cider on their lunch breaks though.

➡ There's always plenty going on – open mic night on Mondays, a quiz on Tuesdays, curries on Thursdays. It's like a Craig David song gone wrong.

⬅ Out the back is this generously proportioned patio area, which provides a welcoming suntrap in which to get started on the pop.

➡ It's at a bit of an odd angle, this picture. One suspects that the photographer has reached the pint of no return and collapsed on the floor in a heap – yet has nonetheless carried on shooting. What a pro.

TERRA NOVA

Mermaid Quay,
Cardiff, CF10 5BZ
029 2045 0947 •
terranovacardiff.com

This Brains-run gaff is the area's pre-eminent bar and quite possibly Cardiff's pointiest building. It's slap in the middle of the snazziest bit of the very-snazzy-indeed end of Cardiff Bay. So there's a lot of snazz around here: not only is Terra Nova ship-shaped, it's also shipshape.

◀ The bar is stocked with a full complement of Brains' cask ales along with more spirits than you can shake a gastric irrigation tube at.

The focus is as much on eating as it is on imbibing alcohol. It's the decor, not the menu, that intrigues though: where else in Cardiff can you see such a distinctive blend of old-fashioned public house and Arabian harem?

There are all sorts of crannies and mezzanine levels. It may be expedient to note that those armchairs are particularly well-placed for the loos.

There's extensive seating on the terrace but, for al fresco ale swilling, your best bet is to head up to the first-floor balconies, which offer both stunning views across the bay and the very real chance that you'll be shat upon by a pigeon.

Y MOCHYN DU

Sophia Close, Pontcanna, Cardiff, CF11 9HW
029 2037 1599 • ymochyndu.com

Y Mochyn Du (The Black Pig) is a funny looking tavern. It's actually an old gatekeeper's lodge at the entrance to Sophia Gardens but appears to have been designed by the Brothers Grimm while taking a quick break from compiling fairy tales about cannibalistic witches.

➧ To the bar, where there's a particular focus on local guest ales, wine, your higher-end lagers and the sort of archaic-looking bottles of sickly liqueurs and spirits – Malibu, Bailey's, Tia Maria – that your parents excavate from their drinks cabinet at Christmas.

What is this obsession with sticking sport-excreting tellies on every available surface? What's wrong with just having a chat?

There's both a conservatory and a large decked area outside so, weather permitting, you've got an embarrassment of seating options.

This feature wall comprises an attempt to replicate Michelangelo's *The Creation of Adam* (perhaps rather better known in its more familiar setting on the ceiling of the Sistine Chapel). Because what's a pint without a slightly cockeyed fresco based on one of the greatest pieces of High Renaissance art ever created?

THE ANEURIN BEVAN

Caerphilly Road, Birchgrove, Cardiff, CF14 4AD
029 2054 4280 • jdwetherspoon.co.uk/home/pubs/the-aneurin-bevan

Here's an idea that seems not so much too good to be true as too true to be good: a branch of Wetherspoon marooned on the Caerphilly Road roundabout at the north end of the Gabalfa flyover that's only accessible by a subway. It sounds like some sort of Ballardian dystopia come to life – albeit one in which you can purchase a beer and burger for £4.99.

➧ There is some irony in naming an outpost of a chain of pubs known for shifting cheap booze by the gallon after the founder of the NHS.

Into the main space (which, oddly, has no bar of its own), where one couple have decided to make a day of watching subtitled rolling news. Well, it gets you out the house, doesn't it?

But if an avalanche of current affairs isn't for you, there's always the opportunity to catch up with a spot of Samuel Pepys instead. "I was in mighty pain all night long of the winde griping of my belly and making of me shit often and vomit too, which is a thing not usual with me," he wrote in July 1666. "But this I impute to the milke that I drank after so much beer." I know the feeling.

O'NEILL'S

20-21 Trinity Street,
Cardiff, CF10 1BH
029 2037 1263 •
oneills.co.uk/trinity-street-in-cardiff

This branch of O'Neill's – known colloquially as Small O'Neill's – is not to be confused with the O'Neill's on St Mary Street. Which is distinguishable by being, well, bigger. Either way, you know what you're going to get: essentially a hostelry from Dublin's Temple Bar fed through a chain pub-shaped filter.

De rigueur Guinness-related ephemera.

There's a bit of history to the place. The Victorian building was previously known as the New Market Hotel and has been a pub for over 100 years. Olivia Newton-John's father Brinley was born here. And, in 2008, the roof was destroyed by a blaze that required 60 firefighters to bring under control while the pub's usual staff were having an away day at Alton Towers. Incredibly, these are all true facts.

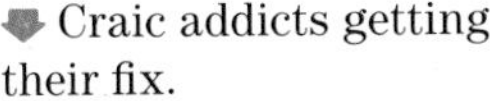

Craic addicts getting their fix.

As well as the various nooks downstairs, there's this separate upstairs bar, which regularly hosts live music. Although how anyone is able to retain the necessary focus to play a musical instrument while faced with the horror of that carpet remains to be seen.

VARSITY

199-201 Richmond Road, Roath, Cardiff, CF24 3BT
029 2048 4480 • smithandjonespubs.com

It's amazing that anyone ever makes it through the door of this branch of Varsity, given how easy it is to be sidetracked by either the Indian restaurant to the left or the dance studio above. Or both – as famously happened with one particularly unfortunate punter. Suffice to say, don't ever attempt to perform an extended Louie Spence-inspired routine having just consumed a large tandoori mixed grill.

Tempting as the offer of a full English breakfast for £1.99 sounds, it's a price point that does force you to consider the provenance of budget sausages – a thought process that really is best avoided.

My notes for Varsity read, in their entirety, "Cheap. Students." But there's plenty to like about the place – there's a sprightly atmosphere and the fact of Brains coming at £1.79 a pint is (quite literally) staggering news.

After a number of alarmingly cheap rounds, the photographer spots the dartboards and decides that he fancies a round of killer. Fortunately, a vigilant member of staff sees him lurching across the room towards the gaming area and promptly confiscates the arrows, fearing that the contest's name may prove to be all too accurate.

THE WOODVILLE

1-5 Woodville Road, Cathays, Cardiff, CF24 4DW
029 2039 7859 • screampubs.co.uk/thewoodvillecardiff

This Scream-owned joint is a student institution. Who knows how many snakebites and black have been downed here over the years. (Do students still drink snakebite and black, or has its evil appeal begun to wane, thanks to the fact that it both sends you a bit loopy and plays havoc with your digestive system?)

◀ There's a veritable chorus line of lagers on offer – they even have Coors Light, possibly the most pointlessly tasteless beer ever conceived (and that's coming from a Foster's drinker).

Christ, there's a lot going on with this decor. Purple armchairs, cushions enveloped in '60s-style fabrics, a halo of coloured light bulbs, bright yellow bunting, a wall painted in a kind of sludge colour and, erm, a hymn board.

Further into the pub and I seem to have reached the mother lode of young people enjoying themselves. By which I mean: trying to drink enough to be able to forget about how long it'll take to repay their student loans.

'Strictly no morris dancing' reads a sign in the beer garden. Although, to be honest, I'm less concerned about the potential for illicit morris dancing than I am about the more pressing issue of the large bottle of mayonnaise that's sitting in direct sunlight.